ry Makers

Martin Luther King

...and the fight for equality

Sarah Ridley

SEA-TO-SEA
Mankato Collingwood London

This edition first published in 2013 by
Sea-to-Sea Publications
Distributed by Black Rabbit Books
P.O. Box 3263, Mankato, Minnesota
56002

Printed in the United States of America,
North Mankato, MN

9 8 7 6 5 4 3 2

Published by arrangement with the
Watts Publishing Group Ltd, London.

Library of Congress Cataloging-in-Publication Data

Ridley, Sarah.
 Martin Luther King-- and the fight for equality /
Sarah Ridley.
    p. cm. -- (History makers)
 Includes index.
 ISBN 978-1-59771-389-4 (library binding)
1. King, Martin Luther, Jr., 1929-1968--Juvenile
literature. 2. African Americans--Biography--Juvenile
literature. 3. African Americans--Civil rights--History-
-20th century--Juvenile literature. 4. Civil rights
workers--United States--Biography--Juvenile literature.
I. Title.
 E185.97.K5R53 2013
 323.092--dc23
 [B]
                        2011049888

Series Editor: Jeremy Smith
Art Director: Jonathan Hair
Design: Simon Morse
Cover Design: Jonathan Hair
Picture Research: Sarah Ridley

Picture credits: AFP/Getty Images:
front cover, 1, 2. AP/Topfoto: 18, 21.
Bettmann/Corbis: 7, 12, 13, 15, 16, 17, 19,
22. Marjory Collins/Bettmann/
Corbis: 6. Raymond Gehman/Corbis:
10. Marvin Koner/Corbis: 14. Bob
Krist/Corbis: 5. Popperfoto/Getty
Images: 20. Flip Schulke/Corbis: 8.
Donald Uhrbrock/Time Life/Getty
Images: 9. Eudora Welty/Corbis: 11.

RD/6000006415/001
May 2012

Contents

The King Family

On January 15, 1929, the
Reverend King and his wife
had a son. They named him
Michael but changed his
name to Martin Luther a
few years later.

1927 ▶	January 15th 1929 ▶
Willie, Martin's sister, is born.	Michael (later Martin Luther) King is born.

MARTIN LUTHER KING, JR.
WAS BORN IN THIS HOUSE
JANUARY 15, 1929

The family lived in a comfortable house in the city of Atlanta, Georgia.

◁ The house where Martin Luther King grew up.

1929 ▶

Worldwide money crisis.

1930 ▶

Alfred, Martin's brother, is born.

To School

As a young boy, Martin played with white and black children. But when it was time to start school, the black children went to one school and the white to another.

A school for African-American children. Usually, these schools were not as good as those for white children.

1935 ▶

Martin starts school.

Gradually, Martin realized that black and white people were treated differently in his country. African-American people even had to sit apart from white people on the bus and use different public washrooms.

1939 ▶

World War II begins in Europe.

The Student

Martin was very smart and he did well at school. He went to college, where he studied to be a church minister, like his father.

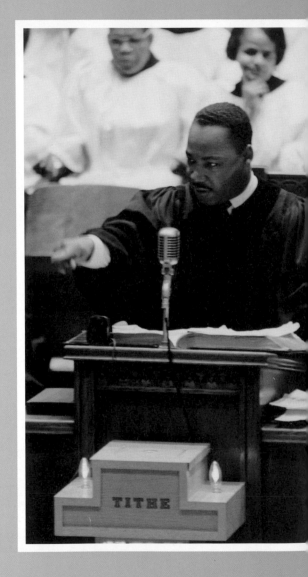

▶ As a student and later on, Martin preached sermons at his father's church.

1944 ▶

Martin goes to Morehouse College in Atlanta, Georgia.

1945 ▶

World War II ends.

During his time at Boston University, he met a young music student named Coretta Scott. They fell in love and were married.

◀ Coretta played the piano. This photo shows her with Martin and two of their children in 1960.

1947 ▶

Martin studies at Crozer Theological Seminary, in Pennsylvania.

1951 ▶

Martin goes to Boston University.

1953 ▶

Martin marries Coretta.

Return to the South

At the age of 25, Martin started a job as pastor at a church in Montgomery, Alabama. A year later, Coretta and Martin had their first baby.

Martin was the pastor of this church in Montgomery.

May
1954 ▶

By law, black and white children should go to the same schools, but many white people stop that from happening.

In the Southern states, life was much harder for black people than in the North. Martin saw that black people had the worst houses, schools, and jobs. They were treated differently from white people in many areas of life.

African-Americans had to use a separate entrance at the movies.

September
1954 ▶

Martin moves to Montgomery, Alabama, to be a pastor.

1955 ▶

The Kings' first child, Yolanda, is born.

Rosa Parks

In December 1955, Martin heard about the arrest of a black woman named Rosa Parks. The Montgomery police arrested her when she refused to give up her bus seat to a white person.

▶ Rosa Parks did not see why she should give up her seat to a white person.

Martin was arrested for his part in the bus protest. Here he walks out of court with Coretta.

The black people of Montgomery asked Martin to lead a protest to show how angry they felt. They stopped using the buses. After a year, the bus company said that black people could sit wherever they liked.

1956 ▶

A bomb is thrown at Martin's home. No one is injured.

1957 ▶

The Kings' second child, Martin Luther King III, is born.

Protest

In 1959, Martin gave up his church job and joined others to fight for equal rights for all African-Americans. He gave speeches, wrote books, led marches, and organized protests.

◀ Despite all this hard work, Martin loved spending time with his children.

1958 ▶

Martin is stabbed in a bookstore.

1959 ▶

Martin steps down from his job as pastor.

Martin believed that all protest should be peaceful, even after someone threw a bomb at his house, and someone else stabbed him. His strong belief in God shone through in his speeches.

Martin's speeches inspired people to join the struggle for fair treatment for African-Americans.

1960 ▶
The King family moves to Atlanta, Georgia.

1961 ▶
The Kings' third child, Dexter, is born.

Birmingham

Birmingham was a city where African-Americans were treated very badly. Martin organized marches to protest against their treatment—and thousands joined him.

Martin was often arrested at protest marches, and went to jail 13 times in total.

1962 ▶

Martin joins the Birmingham protests.

When newspaper photos showed police and firemen attacking the protestors, even more people realized how badly black people were being treated in some parts of the United States.

1963 ▶

The Kings' fourth child, Bernice, is born.

"I Have a Dream"

More and more people wanted to see African-Americans treated fairly. When Martin organized a march in Washington D.C. in 1963, 250,000 people came along.

Martin waves to the crowd at the Washington, D.C. march.

August
1963 ▶

Huge march in America's capital, Washington, D.C.

Martin made his most famous speech at the march. Here is some of it:

"I have a dream that my four little children will one day live in a nation where they will not be judged by the color of their skin but by the content of their character."

November
1963 ▶

President John F. Kennedy is shot dead.

Success at Last

The following year, the U.S. government finally made a law that gave equal rights to all Americans. Black people should now be treated the same as white people in all areas of life.

▲ Martin continued to lead marches and protests to improve the lives of African-Americans.

July **1964** ▶	December **1964** ▶	**1965** ▶
Civil Rights Act becomes law.	Martin receives the Nobel Peace Prize.	Vietnam War begins.

That same year, Martin won the Nobel Peace Prize. This prize is given out each year to the person who is seen to have done the most for peace in the world.

▶ Martin and his Nobel Peace Prize.

1965 ▶

Martin speaks at a huge march in Selma, Alabama.

1965 ▶

Voting Rights Act makes it clear that all people should have the vote.

Death

Sadly, many people did not want to see the changes Martin and others worked toward. In April 1968, Martin was shot by one of these people and died soon afterward.

◀ This photo shows Martin and some friends standing on the same hotel balcony where he was shot.

January
1966 ▶

Martin moves to Chicago.

May
1966 ▶

Martin speaks out against the Vietnam War.

▲ Crowds follow Martin Luther King's coffin through the streets of Atlanta.

Thousands joined the King family at the funeral. Americans continue to commemorate his life on Martin Luther King Day, a federal holiday in January.

April 4th
1968 ▶

Martin Luther King is shot dead.

1986 ▶

Martin Luther King Day becomes a federal holiday.

23

Glossary

Equal rights The same rights for everyone, regardless of their wealth or the color of their skin. Equal rights aim to give people the same chances in life.

Minister/Pastor/Reverend All names for clergymen. They are the people who lead church services and look after the religious needs of the people who live in the area surrounding the church.

World War II (1939-1945) A world war.

Sermon The part of a church service when the minister or pastor gives a religious speech.

Vietnam War (1965-1973) The U.S. Army fought an unsuccessful war in Vietnam. Thousands died.

Vote The right to vote in elections.

Index